I◆I

THE JUDICIARY

I◆I

The Judiciary

**Carl R. Green, Ph.D.,
and William R. Sanford, Ph.D.**

The Rourke Corporation, Inc.

The Rourke Corporation, Inc.
P.O. Box 3328, Vero Beach, FL 32964

Green, Carl R.
  The judiciary / by Carl R. Green and William R. Sanford.
  p. cm. — (American government)
  Includes index.
  Summary: Examines the working of American courts and judicial systems through the eyes of a fictional federal district judge, Duncan Reilly.
  ISBN 0-86593-086-4
  1. Justice, Administration of--United States--Juvenile literature. 2. Courts--United States--Juvenile literature. 3. Judicial process--United States--Juvenile literature. [1. Justice. 2. Courts. 3. Judicial process.] I. Sanford, William R. (William Reynolds), 1927- . II. Title. III. Series.
  KF8700.Z9G74 1990
  347.73'1--dc20
  [347.3071]   90-8670
                                                                                     CIP
                                                                                      AC

Editorial Consultant: Josh M. Fredricks, Judge of the Municipal Court,
    County of Los Angeles, California.
Series Editor: Gregory Lee
Editors: Elizabeth Sirimarco, Marguerite Aronowitz
Book design and production: The Creative Spark,
    Capistrano Beach, CA
Cover photograph: David M. Doody/Tom Stack & Associates

Authors' Note

All descriptions of the workings of the American Government that appear in this book are authentic, as are the citations of historical figures and events. Only the characters who carry the story line are fictional—and we have modeled them as closely as possible upon their real-life counterparts.

Table of Contents

1

The Importance Of The Court System

Duncan Reilly pulled off his black robes and hung them neatly in a small closet. Then he dropped wearily into his swivel chair and rubbed his eyes. "Did I make the right decisions today?" he wondered. "Was justice served in my courtroom?"

The case had been tiring for everyone. The defense attorney had raised objection after objection in a desperate effort to save his client. As the judge presiding in the case, Reilly had been forced to make dozens of rulings. If he'd lost his temper or ruled unfairly, Congressman Peter Scopolus wouldn't have received a fair trial. Had Scopolus violated federal election laws by diverting $600,000 in campaign funds to his own use? According to the jury the answer was "yes." The 12 men and women had brought in a guilty verdict.

Reilly went over the case in his mind. "That's why I'm a federal district judge," he mused. Without the courts, people like Scopolus would make a mockery of the law. The idea made him look up at the framed poster that hung on his wood-paneled wall.

The lettering was childish, for it had been done by his ten-year-old son. The words, however, were central to Reilly's life. "Law," the poster said, "is the set of rules, rights, and obligations that bind a society together." People can't live without laws, Reilly believed. Laws

The blindfolded figure of Lady Justice,
seen in courtrooms throughout the United States, always
carries a scale, representing the weighing of evidence for both sides.

govern our behavior, protect our persons and our property, and guard our freedoms. And judges, he concluded, make sure the laws are enforced fairly.

How old is the rule of law? Reilly remembered Hammurabi's code, a set of laws carved in stone almost 4,000 years ago. What would the Babylonian king think of today's laws? He'd be amazed at how many we need to govern our complex society. Too many to be carved in stone, that's certain.

Reilly's eyes moved to the bronze statue of "Justice" that stood on his desk. The statue was copied from one that stood atop a London courthouse. The blindfolded female figure was shown holding a balance scale in one hand. Reilly often thought of that blindfold when he was judging a case. Judges must be "blind" to everything but the rights and wrongs of the case. In that spirit, Reilly treated every defendant with the same fairness he had shown Congressman Scopolus.

The scales of justice were another important symbol. In the court-room, evidence slowly piled up on both sides of the scales. Sometimes the weight of evidence for or against one side was so clear that decisions were easy to make. At other times, the scales tilted hardly at all. Then it was up to the judge and jury to weigh the evidence fairly so that justice could be served.

Laws Come From Many Sources

Judge Reilly looked at the clock. If he cleared his desk quickly he could still play a set of tennis before supper. He picked up a letter from the top of his "in" basket and groaned. Why had he agreed to talk to the local junior high school history class? Grabbing a yellow legal pad, he swiftly outlined a brief talk on the origins of American law. In one way or another, he wrote, everyone is bound by five types of law. First comes *constitutional law*. All of the basic elements of American government and American freedoms begin with the United States Constitution. The words of the Constitution, however, are open to interpretation. The Bill of Rights guarantees freedom of speech, but how far does that right go? Over the years, the federal courts have defined the limits. For example, no one has the right to yell "Fire!" in

Would You Want To Live Under The Code Of Hammurabi?

King Hammurabi ruled the ancient kingdom of Babylonia almost 4,000 years ago. Hammurabi was a just ruler for his time, but his laws were harsh and inflexible by today's standards. Babylonians couldn't claim to be ignorant of the laws, for they were publicly displayed on a pillar of black stone. The laws below are typical of the "eye-for-an-eye" nature of the 282 laws that made up the Code of Hammurabi.

- If a freeman destroys the eye of another freeman, his own eye shall be destroyed.

- If an innkeeper hears people hatching a plot and does not arrest them, the innkeeper shall be put to death.

- A husband may divorce a childless wife by refunding her dowry and bridal price.

- Those who lease land and do not cultivate it must pay the same rent as that paid by farmers who cultivate their fields properly.

- A man who slanders a woman will be lashed and one-half of his beard will be cut off.

preliminary hearing is not a trial, but a presentation of evidence by prosecutors who want ~e judge to hold a suspect for trial. If the evidence seems sufficient, an arraignment will be scheduled so the accused can enter a plea, arrange bail and receive a trial date.

a crowded theater.

The second type of law is *common law*. This body of custom and tradition began long ago in Great Britain. Traveling judges in the 12th century based their decisions on earlier decisions made in similar cases. This practice became known as the rule of *stare decisis*, Latin for "let the ruling stand." Common law was made up of decisions dealing with property rights, contracts, torts (willful acts that injure another person), and criminal acts. In time, much of the common law was written down and became *statute law*.

Statute law is the body of laws passed by Congress, state legislatures and local governing bodies. Statute laws define the rights and obligations of American citizens. The taxes that pay for government services are established by statute law. If someone challenges the nation's tax laws, the federal courts must decide whether or not the laws are constitutional.

The government also makes *administrative law*. These are the rules federal agencies issue in order to carry out the duties assigned them by Congress. There are actually more administrative laws on the books than there are statute laws. Do you want to operate a ham radio transmitter? The rules governing their operation are written by the Federal Communications Commission, not by Congress.

Finally there's the *law of equity*. Like the common law, equity is based on earlier decisions. Typically, it provides a means of preventing an injustice when statute law doesn't apply. Perhaps the Air Force wants to set up a bombing range next to a rancher's property. The rancher protests that the noise would stampede his cattle. It would be my job, Reilly was thinking, to listen to both sides so I could determine what was fair. If I agreed with the rancher, I could issue a legal order (an *injunction*) forbidding the use of the bombing range.

The notes filled two pages. That's good stuff, but it won't excite the students, he decided. I'll have to pep up my talk with some stories of what it's really like to be a federal district judge.

Balancing The Legislative And Executive Branches

The talk went better than Judge Reilly had expected. The class of

The law is a complex body of words and ideas refined, collected and redefined by the courts year after year. The laws "on the books" in cities, counties and states fills countless libraries and databases nationwide.

eighth graders listened intently to his explanation of the law and how it applied to their lives. After about 20 minutes of speaking, Reilly reached a stopping place and asked for questions. Hands shot into the air. He pointed to a red-haired girl in the front row.

"We've been studying the Constitution," she said. "Can you tell us how the judicial branch is able to check the executive and legislative branches?"

Reilly smiled. He guessed the teacher had planted that question to get things started.

The nation's founders, he explained, designed a government with three branches. The legislative branch makes the laws and the executive branch administers them. It's up to the judicial branch to interpret them. In order to safeguard our democracy, each branch is given the power to "check" the other two. Thus, no one branch can overpower the other two.

The Constitution, Reilly continued, devotes only three short sections to the judicial branch. By contrast, the legislative branch receives almost six times as much space. The founders simply outlined the court system and left it up to Congress to fill in the details. Except for giving lifetime jobs to federal judges, the mechanism for checking the power of the other two branches was not spelled out.

"But our teacher told us that the judicial branch is the equal of the other two branches," a boy said.

"Your teacher is right," Reilly agreed, "but the courts didn't gain their equal status right away. The honor of making the judicial branch the equal of the other branches belongs to John Marshall. He was the fourth Chief Justice of the Supreme Court. In 1803, in the case of *Marbury v. Madison*, he ruled that the federal courts could declare that a law was unconstitutional. Today we call that the right of judicial review."

A hand was waving at the back of the room. "Judge Reilly," a girl called out, "does that mean the courts could review something our principal might do?"

"Yes, it certainly does," Reilly assured her. "If you believe the principal has violated your rights, you can take the matter to court. If the court agrees with you, the principal must back down. Our system of checks and balances really does work to protect both our rights and our democratic system."

Federal Courts And State Courts

The questions shifted to the criminal cases over which Judge Reilly had presided. He told them about the trials of tax evaders, drug dealers, and a famous kidnapper. "Did you find them all guilty?" a boy yelled.

"That's not my job," Reilly said with a laugh. "My job is to see that the accused receive a fair trial. It's the jury's job to decide on their guilt or innocence. The right to a jury trial is guaranteed by the Constitution."

"My brother has to go to court for reckless driving," a freckle-faced girl said. "I hope he gets you for a judge."

"That's kind of you," Reilly smiled, "but traffic cases are only heard in state courts. Remember that the federal government only has those powers spelled out in the Constitution. All other powers are reserved for the states and their local governments."

He explained that his court was limited to cases involving federal laws and regulations. The technical term for the right to hear a particular case is *jurisdiction*. When the federal courts don't have jurisdiction, cases must be tried in the state courts.

"If your brother broke a federal law, he could be tried in my courtroom," Reilly continued. "Let's imagine that he threw a rotten tomato at the president. That would earn him a date in a federal court." The class laughed at the thought of anyone being foolish enough to throw a tomato at the president.

Reilly drew a diagram on the chalkboard. Both the state and federal judicial systems have lower courts and higher courts, he explained. A case is assigned to a particular court according to the nature of the crime or the dispute. "Your brother's case will be heard in traffic court," he said. "Youthful offenders are tried in juvenile courts. More serious offenses, such as armed robbery, are tried in municipal or superior courts."

The federal district courts hear over 275,000 cases a year in more

The jurors here lean forward to better view an exhibit—
a physical piece of evidence submitted during a trial to support either the
prosecution or defense.
Here the jurors examine a scale model of a crime scene.

than 90 district courts. These courts serve the 50 states, the District of Columbia, Puerto Rico, and the island territories. The government also provides special-purpose courts, such as tax courts and tariff courts. In the federal judicial system, the courts of appeals are directly above the district courts. This means that someone who loses a case in the district court can ask the court of appeals to review it. But the appeals court will only accept a case if it appears that the lower court acted improperly. Appeals lost there can be further appealed to the U.S. Supreme Court.

"How many federal district judges are there?" a boy asked.

"I am one of just over 500 district judges," Reilly said. "I feel very proud to have a seat on the federal bench."

2

The Making Of A Judge

The morning mail brought a letter with a familiar postmark and return address. Duncan Reilly looked at it and felt a faint sense of shock. The years were flying by too quickly—his high school class was about to celebrate its big 25-year reunion.

Reilly shoved aside the court papers he'd been reading and picked up his pen. The reunion committee had enclosed a questionnaire that asked for the history of each class member since graduation. Reilly began to fill in the blanks.

College: Tyler Junior College
(Associate of Arts)
Rice University
(Bachelor of Arts)
Graduate School: University of Texas Law School
(Doctor of Laws)

Counting elementary school and high school, that was 21 years of schooling, Reilly realized. "I've been going to classes nearly half my life!" At times he had trouble remembering his early college years, but law school was vivid in his memory. He could still hear Dean

*Before a judge passes a sentence the convicted person
is always allowed to make a statement.*

Shockley's voice on that hectic first day. "Take a good look at the people sitting next to you," she had said. "Many of them won't be here next year."

The prediction had been accurate. Even though the students were all hand-picked, the failure rate was high. Reilly shuddered as he remembered the score of 63 he'd earned on his first exam in Contract Law. "That was the first D I'd ever received," he thought. "It sure caught my attention."

A change in study habits saved Reilly's law career. As he read the dozens of cases assigned to the students each week, he summarized each one on index cards. Reviewing the cards kept the cases fresh in his mind. Soon, like a well-exercised muscle, his memory for detail improved. Reilly also learned to pick out the important facts in a case so that he could relate them to earlier cases.

During the summers Reilly had worked as a law clerk for a firm that represented big oil companies. He spent long days checking dusty land records in the county courthouse. Then his boss moved him to the immense law library to research old cases. The other lawyers in the office praised his work, but Reilly thought his assignments were boring.

By his third year, Reilly was earning straight As. His improved grades won him the right to work on the school law review journal. But his real joy came when he argued cases in mock trials organized by his professors. His first taste of courtroom life convinced Reilly that he'd found his place in the law.

From Law Office To The Judge's Bench

Graduating from law school was just the first step. Before he could practice law, Reilly had to first pass the state's bar exam. When friends teased him about "passing the bar," he explained that "bar" refers to the area in an English court that only judges and lawyers are allowed to enter.

The three-day exam tested his knowledge of the law to the utmost. Half of the test was made up of difficult multiple choice questions and the other half required long essay answers. Despite cram courses and weeks of study, many of his classmates failed. Their only hope was to try again in six months.

For Duncan Reilly, the news was good. He passed on his first try. His proud parents ordered business cards for him. The fine engraving read, "Duncan E. Reilly, Attorney at Law."

The years that followed were busy ones. Reilly joined a well-known law firm and specialized in courtroom work. He made a name for himself as a hard-working defense attorney in criminal cases. Along the way he also handled civil cases that were mostly divorces and personal injury suits.

The courtroom proceedings in a civil trial do not differ greatly from criminal trials: witnesses give testimony, lawyers cross-examine them, and physical evidence is exhibited for the benefit of both a judge and (if there is one) jury.

As his skills increased, so did his income. He was invited to become a partner in a large Houston firm. The future looked bright, but Reilly felt restless. He became more aware of the judges in whose courtrooms he appeared. The good ones were masters of the art of safeguarding the rights of all who appeared before them. Reilly decided that he'd like to be a federal judge.

As he did everything else, Reilly planned his strategy with care. Neither the Constitution nor statute law listed any specific qualifications for federal judges. Just as a president appoints the justices of the Supreme Court, he also appoints judges to the federal appeals courts and district courts. Each appointment must also be confirmed by the Senate.

The American judicial system is made up of state and federal courts. The state courts hear cases arising under state law. The federal courts hold jurisdiction over criminal cases and civil suits arising under federal law. Appeals of lower court decisions are taken to the courts of

State Courts

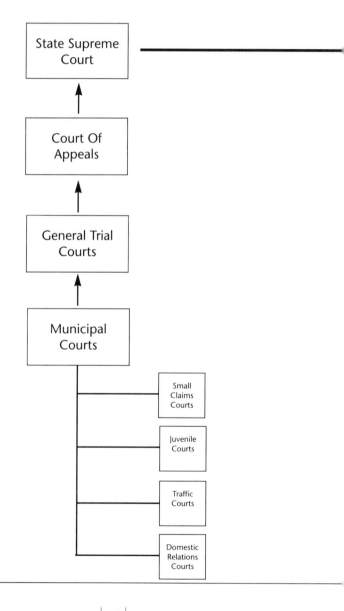

appeals. If a constitutional question is involved, the U.S. Supreme Court serves as the ultimate court of appeals. Its decision is final—until the law is changed by Congress or until the court reverses itself.

Federal Courts

```
                    ┌──────────────┐         ┌──────────────┐
──────────▶         │ U.S. Supreme │ ◀────── │  Court Of    │
                    │    Court     │         │Military Appeals│
                    └──────────────┘         └──────────────┘
                          ▲
                          │
                    ┌──────────────┐         ┌──────────────┐
                    │ U.S. Court   │         │  Court Of    │
                    │ Of Appeals   │         │ Appeals For  │
                    └──────────────┘         │ The Federal  │
                      ▲    ▲                  │   Circuit    │
                      │    │                  └──────────────┘
                    ┌──────────────┐
                    │ U.S. District│                ▲
                    │   Courts     │                │
                    └──────────────┘         ┌────────────┐
                                             │ Court Of   │
                                             │International│
                                             │   Trade    │
                    ┌──────────┐             └────────────┘
                    │ Tariff   │             ┌────────────┐
                    │ Court    │             │  Court     │
                    └──────────┘             │   Of       │
                                             │  Claims    │
                    ┌──────────┐             └────────────┘
                    │  Tax     │
                    │ Court    │
                    └──────────┘
```

Legend

──────────▶   Line of Appeal

---------▶   Limited Appeal Privileges

☐   Lower or special courts

☐   General or Appeals Courts

A good attorney often must ask some difficult questions when confronting a witness.

How do you obtain a presidential appointment? First, Reilly knew, he or she had to be a highly competent attorney. He hoped he was qualified in that respect. Second, it helps if one belongs to the president's political party. Presidents seldom appoint judges who reflect an opposing political philosophy. To gain exposure, Reilly volunteered to serve on his party's campaign committee. In the next four years he would have the opportunity to play a major role in electing a popular mayor and a U.S. senator.

When the time seemed right, Reilly let party leaders know he was available. Beyond that, there wasn't much else he could do. If he campaigned too loudly, he would almost certainly ruin his chances.

Reilly waited patiently as he continued working as a defense attorney. When an elderly judge died of a heart attack, Reilly knew he had a chance at being considered for the vacant bench, but he also knew he wasn't the only person who wanted a judgeship. After two long weeks, the hoped-for phone call came through. His friend, Senator Chase, had suggested Reilly's name to the White House.

The Road To Confirmation

A court clerk bustled in and handed Reilly an armload of papers. "We've got a busy day ahead of us," she said.

Reilly looked up from the questionnaire and frowned at the papers. The caseload was overwhelming at times. But he never regretted his decision to put on the black robes of a judge.

With a sigh he returned to the questionnaire. After "job currently held," he wrote, "Federal District Judge." As he did so, he thought again of the hard road that led to that title. Thanks to the custom of "senatorial courtesy," the president had accepted Senator Chase's recommendation. The White House didn't often pick fights with senators over district court appointments. But candidates still had to be screened before the president sent their names to the Senate for confirmation.

First, the F.B.I. gave Reilly a routine security check. No one wanted to appoint federal judges who had a history of poor judgment or shady business dealings. After that, two White House officials visited

Reilly in Houston.

The intense young staffers quizzed him on all the important national issues. They reminded Reilly that his appointment would be for life unless he resigned or was impeached for misconduct. By appointing judges who shared his views the president could influence the nation long after leaving office. Of course, federal judges aren't bound by their former positions. In his short time on the bench, Reilly had already changed his views on capital punishment. After reading the favorable staff report the president nominated Duncan Reilly to fill the district court vacancy. That left two final hurdles. First, the American Bar Association's Committee on the Federal Judiciary had to evaluate his fitness to serve as a district judge. Members of the committee checked into his judicial temperament, his legal experience, his character, and his intelligence. After a careful grilling, the committee rated Reilly as "well qualified."

Next came the Senate confirmation hearings. Reilly appeared before the Judiciary Committee and answered the same questions all over again. The committee also called witnesses who testified as to his character and legal experience. Afterward, Reilly felt as though he'd been run through a wringer. But he also knew that candidates for the Supreme Court were treated much more roughly.

The Judiciary Committee issued a favorable report and both Texas senators spoke in Reilly's behalf. Thanks to their support, the Senate voted 89-0 to give its "advice and consent" to the appointment. The long wait was over. Duncan Reilly was now a federal judge.

The Judge's Role

As a lawyer, Reilly's job had been to protect the interests of his clients. Each case was a test of his ability to outthink and outtalk the opposing lawyers. In the heat of a courtroom argument he couldn't always worry about right and wrong.

As a judge, he saw the law in a different light. The cases that came to his courtroom reflected all of the stresses of a rapidly changing society. A single decision could affect an individual, a city, or the entire nation. There were federal judges who ordered the schools in

Photography used to be prohibited in most courtrooms
until the 1980s, even though trials must be open to the public.
Sketches like this were the only way to offer visuals with news stories.
Now many judicial proceedings are televised and videotaped.

Kansas City, Boston, and other cities to use busing to achieve racial integration. It was a federal judge who gave the go-ahead for the construction of the Alaska pipeline. And it was a federal judge who ordered better patient care in Alabama's mental hospitals.

Reilly soon found out how much he didn't know. He turned to *The Judge's Bench Book* in order to learn courtroom procedures. After his confirmation he attended seminars put on by the Federal Judicial Center. Along with the techniques of managing a courtroom, Reilly absorbed a larger lesson. He learned never to forget that he held people's lives and fortunes in his hands.

Like all district courts, Judge Reilly's court held *original jurisdiction*. That meant that any civil or criminal case filed under federal law is first heard in a district court. Reilly tried criminal cases that ranged from bank robbery and kidnapping to mail fraud and counterfeiting. The civil cases often involved lawsuits arising under the tax, labor, and commercial laws of the United States.

"Would you choose a different career if you were starting over?" the questionnaire concluded. Reilly printed NO in firm letters. He didn't miss the long hours and the agony of lost cases that went with his law practice. On the other hand, he did miss his six-figure income. Many successful lawyers earned three times his judge's salary, which was set by Congress. To make up for the lower income, he had security and regular hours. Just as importantly, he enjoyed the prestige that the American people give their judges.

He recalled his first day in court. As he entered the wood-paneled courtroom the bailiff had called out, "All rise." Instantly, everyone stood up. Reilly stood behind the judge's bench and waited for someone to sit down. No one did. It was a long moment before he realized that the entire courtroom was waiting for him to take his seat.

3

Bringing A Criminal Case To Court

As Reilly finished the questionnaire, his clerk peeked in through the door. The workday was starting and Sally Price looked a little impatient.

"Sally, what's on the docket this morning?" Reilly asked. "You're scheduled to hear *United States v. Farnham*," she replied. "That's the case of the young man who allegedly broke into the post office stamp machine. He's charged with damaging the machine and running off with $300 worth of stamps."

Reilly looked over the briefing papers. A defendant had once told him that the formal title of her case made her feel as though the whole country was prosecuting her. In fact, it simply meant that she was being tried for breaking a federal law.

"I see that Fran Jerome is defending," Reilly said. "Farnham is lucky to have her. She's one of the public defenders who really does her homework. But she's drawn Bill Ryan as prosecutor. Our bright assistant district attorney is anxious to make a name for himself. He won't give Fran an inch."

Fran Jerome had been assigned to the case soon after Farnham's arrest. The young man had been taken before the same U.S. magistrate who had issued the warrant for his arrest. Magistrate Holly Janeway informed the accused of his rights. Then she asked Farnham if he wanted a lawyer. Farnham said he did, but that he couldn't afford one.

Under the Criminal Justice Act, that entitled him to a public defender. Some defenders were volunteers, but helping poor clients was Jerome's only job. Her fees were set by law, so she wasn't getting rich.

Janeway had also considered the question of bail. At one time Farnham would have been held in jail if he couldn't guarantee his return to court by posting bail in cash. Defendants who didn't have the cash had to pay a bail bond company to put up the money. Under the 1966 Bail Reform Act, however, the federal courts no longer required cash bail from nonviolent suspects. Farnham was set free after giving his word that he would return for his preliminary hearing.

Some suspects don't get off that cheaply. In a case involving tax fraud, Reilly had once set a businessman's bail at $2 million. The man had already moved much of his money to Brazil, and Reilly guessed that he was planning to follow it. He hoped the high bail would convince the suspect that he had to show up for his trial. If he didn't, the government was entitled to keep the $2 million.

The Preliminary Hearing

Fran Jerome had filed a pre-trial motion to dismiss the case. Stripped of its legal language, her argument had been simply to ask for dismissal on the grounds that there wasn't enough evidence to convict her client.

Magistrate Janeway had then scheduled a preliminary hearing to test the strength of the evidence. Judge Reilly thought of these hearings as mini-trials. They could lead either to an arraignment (a court appearance during which the suspect enters a plea of guilty or not guilty), or to a dismissal of the charges.

Because preliminary hearings do not require a jury, the courtroom was almost empty. The official staff consisted of the clerk of the court, a court reporter, and a uniformed officer called the bailiff. The two attorneys were waiting when Janeway entered the room. At her signal the bailiff left and returned a moment later with Henry Farnham. The magistrate hardly recognized the defendant. Jerome had insisted that he wear a suit as a gesture of respect for the court.

Bill Ryan summed up the government's evidence. The prosecutor described Farnham's encounter with the stamp machine, which had

Every court has a clerk and a reporter near the judge's bench who keep track of every trial detail by transcribing all testimony, cataloging exhibits, and managing all paperwork so that the courtroom proceedings are smooth.

apparently accepted the young man's money without giving him any stamps. Ryan said he had two witnesses who would swear that they'd heard Farnham threaten to "get even" with the post office. Furthermore, a witness had seen the accused running away from the damaged stamp machine the night of the crime. The federal marshal who made the arrest testified that he'd found a crowbar in Farnham's car. Paint chips on the crowbar matched the paint from the stamp machine.

Fran Jerome didn't dispute the evidence. Instead, she tried to convince Magistrate Janeway that no one would profit by continuing the prosecution of *United States v. Farnham*. Her client, she told the judge, was ready to pay for any damages he'd caused. He never had any criminal intent, she concluded.

Janeway had listened carefully and examined the evidence. She had kicked a few vending machines herself and felt some sympathy for Farnham. But people couldn't be allowed to attack federal property just because it didn't work properly. Also, there was the matter of the missing stamps. If Farnham had taken them, that went well beyond "getting even."

"Ms. Jerome," Janeway said, "does your client waive his right to be indicted by the grand jury?" If the defense attorney had said yes, the case could have moved directly to arraignment. Instead, she shook her head.

The magistrate turned to the prosecuting attorney. "Mr. Ryan," she said, "take this case to the grand jury. Ask them if there are grounds to issue an indictment of Mr. Farnham."

Indictment And Arraignment

Ten days later, Bill Ryan took his case to the grand jury. Unlike a trial jury, a grand jury doesn't decide guilt or innocence. Its only job is to decide whether an accused should be brought to trial. In the Farnham case, the grand jury listened to the evidence and quickly returned an *indictment.*

After the indictment was issued, Farnham appeared in Judge Reilly's court for his *arraignment.* Like his right to a public defender, the arraignment was based on Sixth Amendment rights. All defendants are entitled to speedy trials and the right to know the charge filed against them.

After Bill Ryan had presented the two charges of theft and vandalism, Farnham had entered his plea. Up until this moment, Reilly had expected a *plea bargain*. Normally, he disliked these deals in which a defense attorney trades a guilty plea for a conviction on a lesser charge. With so many cases clogging the courts, the prosecution often accepts the bargain in order to avoid a time-consuming trial. But critics say that plea bargaining puts pressure on defendants. Guilty people may escape severe punishment this way, and innocent people may plead guilty rather than risk going to trial.

Jerome had already approached Bill Ryan to suggest a plea bargain. Ryan agreed to accept a guilty plea on a lesser charge: vandalism of federal property. He didn't see much sense in wasting more time on the case.

According to the plea bargain, Farnham was supposed to enter a guilty plea. But he surprised everyone by saying, "Not guilty, your honor." Reilly had questioned him closely. Did Farnham understand the consequences of his plea? If a jury found him guilty, the judge warned, he could be sent to prison for a year and fined $10,000.

Farnham stuck to his decision. In a low voice, he said, "I want my day in court."

After that, only the question of bail remained. Farnham had returned for his arraignment, but would he now flee to avoid a trial? Would he be a danger to other people if he were set free? Reilly decided that the answer to both questions was "no."

"Will you promise to return for your trial?" he asked.

Farnham looked surprised. "Of course I will," he said. "I want the jury to hear my side of the story."

Before Reilly could set a date for the trial, Jerome asked for a *continuance*. She said she needed time to prepare her case. Reilly granted her a three-week delay.

The Defense Builds Its Case

The three weeks of the continuance passed swiftly. Fran Jerome used the time to *subpoena* witnesses and to consult with her client. The subpoenas were court orders that told witnesses they would be required to testify.

Jerome's meetings with Henry Farnham took place in her tiny

Defendants who go on trial in criminal cases are risking their freedom, their fortunes and—in a few cases—their lives. The average spectator caught up in the drama focuses on the judge, the jury, and the witnesses. A look at the program, however, reveals that all trials have large casts. Here is a typical cast list, in alphabetical order:

The Player	The Player's Role
Bailiff	The court's sergeant-at-arms. The bailiff swears in witnesses, preserves order in the courtroom, and guards the privacy of the jury while it's making its decision.
Clerk of the Court	The court's secretary. The clerk of the court keeps track of all the paperwork relating to the trial. This includes case records, exhibits and evidence, depositions, and subpoenas.
Court Reporter	The court's recorder. The court reporter uses a stenotype machine to take down a word-for-word record of everything said during the trial. The stenotype tape is later used to prepare a complete transcript of each day's testimony.

You Can't Tell The Players Without A Program

Defendant   In a criminal trial, the person whose guilt or innocence is being decided. In a civil case, the person (or company) being sued by the plaintiff.

Lawyers   The attorneys who represent the opposing sides. A defense attorney represents the defendant in both criminal and civil trials. A prosecutor presents the case against the defendant in a criminal trial.

Judge   The courtroom's "director." The judge explains and interprets the law, instructs the jury, and rules on matters of evidence and testimony.

Jury   A panel of citizens drawn at random from the community. The jury weighs the evidence and decides for or against the defendant in a criminal trial. In a civil suit, the jury chooses a winner in the conflict between the plaintiff and the defendant.

Plaintiff   The injured party in a civil suit. The plaintiff has come to court in an attempt to collect damages from the defendant.

Witnesses   People called to testify under oath. Witnesses sometimes emerge as "stars" when the case is decided by their testimony.

Testimony given by witnesses is a major part of most trials, and judge and jury must weigh the strength of the evidence presented by witnesses.

office. Despite the evidence, Farnham claimed that he had not intended to rob the post office.

"Run that by me again," Jerome said.

Farnham's face took on a stubborn look. "That stamp machine ripped me off," he told her. "I was just getting even."

I have a crazy man for a client, the attorney told herself. She looked over the file she was building. As the defense attorney, she had access to all the evidence collected by the prosecution. She reread the reports of the arresting officers and statements taken from witnesses.

At first glance, the facts seemed to guarantee a guilty verdict. Farnham had charged into the post office in the morning, demanding to see the postmaster. A clerk had listened to his complaint that the stamp machine had "stolen" his eight quarters. Then he'd given

Farnham a complaint form to fill out. Farnham pounded his fist on the counter and demanded immediate action. The clerk told him to come back later.

Farnham had come back to the post office that night. He didn't deny that, nor did he deny that he'd broken into the stamp machine. He did deny that he'd taken the missing stamps.

"I only took eight 25-cent stamps," he insisted. "That's what the machine owed me. When the jury hears that, they'll understand. No one likes to be ripped off by a machine."

"You're lucky this case is being heard by Judge Reilly," Jerome said. "He's as fair as they come and he tries hard to fit the punishment to the crime. If you're convicted, we may be able to convince him that you don't deserve a prison sentence."

Farnham flared up. "You've already given up on me," he snapped. "If you don't want to defend me, just say so. I'll act as my own defense attorney."

The thought of Henry Farnham matching wits with Bill Ryan made Jerome laugh. "Calm down," she said in a friendlier voice. "We have a saying in my business: 'A man who serves as his own attorney has a fool for a client.'"

Farnham said he was sorry and he asked Jerome to stay on the case. They shook hands and began planning their strategy for the trial.

4

The Criminal Trial

Judge Reilly entered his courtroom at the stroke of ten on a hot Tuesday morning. "All rise," the bailiff called out. There was a moment of silence as Reilly took his place behind the high judge's bench. Then, at his nod, everyone else sat down.

From her place at the clerk's table, Sally Price announced that the court would hear the case of *United States v. Farnham.* Reilly greeted the two attorneys and the defendant. Then he asked the bailiff to remove the witnesses from the courtroom. He didn't want them to hear anything that might influence their testimony.

When the bailiff returned, Reilly asked him to bring in the jury panel. A moment later, 40 men and women filed in and took seats at the back of the courtroom. Reilly told them that the clerk would draw 12 of their names at random.

Price called out the names. Seven men and five women took their seats in the jury box. The judge explained that the jurors should tell the court their names, addresses, and occupations. Unless they lived alone, he also wanted to know what their spouses and children did for a living. "Please don't feel upset if you're dismissed," he said. "No one in this court is questioning your character."

Almost at once, Reilly dismissed a juror whose wife worked for the post office. He wasn't sure the man could be impartial in a case

A murder defendant is secured in chains and handcuffs for extra security and escorted by several bailiffs into a courtroom.

Every second of the day and night Americans fall victim to felony crimes. Overworked police officers answer the 911 calls and begin their journey through their search for suspects. After

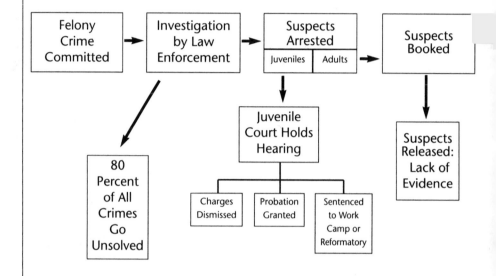

Felony Crime Committed → Investigation by Law Enforcement → Suspects Arrested (Juveniles | Adults) → Suspects Booked

80 Percent of All Crimes Go Unsolved

Juvenile Court Holds Hearing → Charges Dismissed | Probation Granted | Sentenced to Work Camp or Reformatory

Suspects Released: Lack of Evidence

arrests are made, the slow journey through the judicial system begins. The process shown here is typical of both the state and federal courts.

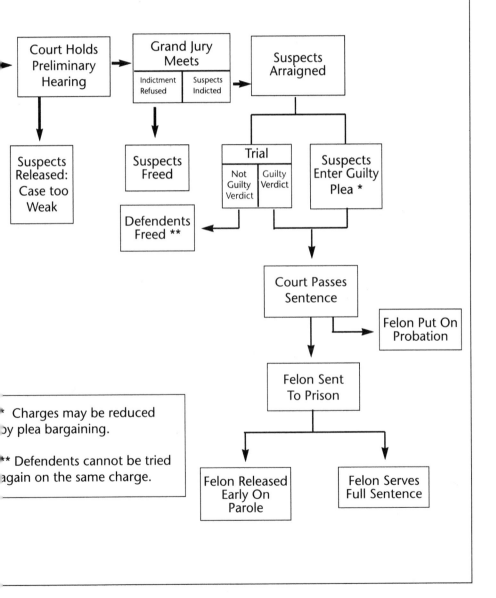

Court Holds Preliminary Hearing

Grand Jury Meets
| Indictment Refused | Suspects Indicted |

Suspects Arraigned

Suspects Released: Case too Weak

Suspects Freed

Trial
| Not Guilty Verdict | Guilty Verdict |

Suspects Enter Guilty Plea *

Defendents Freed **

Court Passes Sentence

Felon Put On Probation

Felon Sent To Prison

* Charges may be reduced by plea bargaining.

** Defendents cannot be tried again on the same charge.

Felon Released Early On Parole

Felon Serves Full Sentence

that involved his wife's place of work. Another juror was called to take the man's place.

When Reilly was satisfied, he turned the questioning over to Bill Ryan and Fran Jerome. Some federal judges, he knew, did all the questioning themselves—and a few let the attorneys do it all. Ryan and Jerome had their questions ready. Did the jurors know anyone involved in the case? Had they formed an opinion about the case? Had they ever been arrested? The questions went on and on.

Two of the jurors were convinced that anyone arrested for a crime was probably guilty. The defense asked Reilly to dismiss them *for cause*. A moment later the prosecutor used two *preemptory challenges*. With this type of challenge he didn't have to explain his reasons for dismissing two young women. Judge Reilly guessed that Ryan was trying to weed out jurors who might feel overly sorry for the defendant.

Another juror was called to replace each juror who was excused. After an hour of questions, 12 jurors and two alternates were ready to be sworn in. The oath they swore bound them to set aside their personal prejudices and judge the evidence fairly.

Are Jury Trials Worth The Effort?

With the jury seated, the trial was ready to begin. Judge Reilly looked at the clock and announced a recess. He hoped to catch up on some paperwork while everyone else was eating lunch.

Just as Reilly took his first bite of sandwich, however, Joe Torres walked into the judge's chambers. Reilly sighed and pushed his second sandwich toward the newspaper reporter.

"Thanks, Judge," Torres said good-naturedly. "I'm doing a series on the jury system," he explained between mouthfuls. "The title will be, 'Has the jury system outlived its usefulness?'"

"The Constitution doesn't think so," Reilly observed.

Torres smiled and made a note. He could always count on Reilly for some good quotes. The reporter already knew the technical side of jury selection. Court officials made up lists of possible jurors and delivered them to the clerk of the court. The names were taken from voter lists, tax rolls, and other official records. According to federal law, the people chosen must represent a cross-section of the commu-

An Illinois jury (with 12 jurors and six alternates) is escorted to the courtroom to begin hearing a trial. Sometimes it takes days to select a jury of citizens who have not formed opinions about the case they will hear.

nity. That meant that a jury should be made up of all ages, races and occupations.

Before the court begins a new term, the clerk sends a summons to each prospective juror. The summons tells the juror to report for duty on a specific date. Those who have good reasons for not serving can ask to be excused. The people most often excused are the self-employed, the disabled, the ill, and the parents of small children. People who ignore the summons are liable to arrest.

"Forget the Constitution for a moment," Torres said at last. "Why don't we let the judges decide on a defendant's guilt or innocence?

Most jurors don't know anything about the law."

Reilly shook his head. "Jury trials are part of the democratic tradition," he said. "The ancient Greeks used juries, and in Great Britain even the Normans used 12-man juries to settle land disputes. In 1215, nobles were guaranteed jury trials by the Magna Carta. And some sixty years later, parliament extended the right to the common people."

"Should we keep a custom just because it's old?" Torres asked.

"The British tried to deny American colonists the right to jury trials," Reilly responded. "That was a major cause of the Revolutionary War. The right to be judged by a jury of your peers is written into the Constitution and the Bill of Rights. It's also guaranteed by the states. The reasons are easy to see.

"First, the people on a jury use their common sense to make decisions based on what they believe is right. They cut through legal tangles and get to the heart of the matter. Second, the jury system helps the judiciary check the tendency of government officials to abuse their own power. Many a politician has gone to jail after being indicted by a grand jury and convicted by a trial jury."

The Trial

Henry Farnham's trial started promptly at two o'clock. Judge Reilly asked the clerk to read the charges against the defendant. Then he looked at the two attorneys. "Are you ready to present your opening arguments?" he asked.

Bill Ryan stood up, turned to the jury, and outlined the prosecution's case. The assistant federal attorney described the damaged stamp machine and the missing stamps. Some of the jurors made notes as he talked. All listened intently.

When Ryan sat down, Fran Jerome described the defense's case. She emphasized that Farnham had never been in trouble with the law before. She ended by saying that she would prove that her client had not stolen the missing stamps.

Ryan then called five witnesses to the stand. Two middle-aged women pointed to Farnham and said they'd heard him threaten to "get even." A postal clerk described Farnham as "out of control" when he made his complaint. The clerk said that the problem could have been worked out if the young man had been a little more patient. A grey-haired woman followed the clerk to the witness stand. She pointed to Farnham as the man she'd seen running away from the damaged stamp machine the night of the crime. Finally, a federal marshal described the paint chips he'd found on Farnham's crowbar. Ryan showed the crowbar to the jury and asked that it be labeled as Exhibit A.

Jerome cross-examined each witness after Ryan finished. She couldn't shake their stories, but they did agree that Farnham hadn't threatened to harm anyone. The postal clerk also admitted that the stamp machine had a long record of breakdowns.

After Ryan rested his case, the defense presented its side. Jerome called several witnesses who testified to Farnham's good character. Then, with the air of someone pulling a rabbit out of a hat, she called a second post office official.

"My client is accused of stealing stamps," she said to the woman. "Is there another explanation for the missing stamps?"

The woman looked embarrassed, but her voice was steady. "After you visited my office last week, I did an inventory of all our stamps," she said. "I discovered a clerical error. The 'missing' stamps were never loaded into the machine."

With that, Jerome offered the post office account sheets as Exhibit B. Ryan cross-examined the witness but failed to shake her story.

Confident now, Jerome put Henry Farnham on the stand. He told the court that he'd been out of work and that two dollars was a lot of money to him. He said that he was sorry now, but that the clerk's rude treatment had enraged him.

Farnham looked directly at the jury. "The machine ripped me off and the post office didn't care," he said. "I truly believed that I had the right to take my eight stamps, even if it meant breaking into the machine."

The Jury Returns Its Verdict

Ryan put Farnham through a long cross-examination. The prosecutor tried to force the defendant to admit that he'd intended to steal both money and stamps. Farnham shook his head and stuck to his

All juries are made up of one's "peers"—American citizens of all backgrounds who will listen to the evidence presented during a trial and give a verdict.

story.

With the testimony completed, the attorneys presented their closing arguments. Ryan reviewed the evidence and told the jury that it was their job to convict Henry Farnham. "If you don't," he warned, "you'll be telling any hothead who comes along that it's okay to break into government property." Jerome stressed the bad luck that led Farnham to make a choice he now regretted. "It's not your job to reform society," she said. "It is your job to judge the defendant fairly."

Judge Reilly then gave his instructions to the jury. He defined "attempted theft" and "vandalism of government property." "You must decide beyond a reasonable doubt whether or not Henry Farnham committed either of those acts," he said. "Remember that our society provides legal ways for people to recover property. Taking the law into one's own hands is not one of them."

Reilly also told the jury that they must return a unanimous verdict. A vote of 11-1 wasn't good enough. If that one juror didn't change his or her vote, the result would be a *hung* jury. Without a verdict, the entire case would have to be retried. Whatever their verdict, no one would know what went on in the jury room unless they chose to speak out after the trial.

Once they reached the jury room, the 12 people quickly elected Marta Polenski as foreman. Polenski passed out slips of paper and asked each person to vote on each charge. On the charge of attempted theft, the vote was 10-2 for a "not guilty" verdict. On the charge of vandalism, the vote was 8-4 for "guilty."

One by one, the members of the jury explained their votes. The two people who voted "guilty" on the theft admitted that they hadn't fully understood the charge. When they were reminded that the missing stamps had been found, they changed their votes. A second vote found Farnham not guilty of attempted theft.

On the second charge, several jury members said they felt sorry for the defendant. Polenski reminded them that they weren't social workers. "Did he vandalize the stamp machine? Was it wrong for him to do so?" she asked. "If the answer is 'yes' to both questions, we must find him guilty."

That argument swung the guilty vote on the second charge to 12-0. A juror called the bailiff and he escorted them back to the courtroom. With Henry Farnham watching nervously, Polenski stood and read the verdict. "We find the defendant, Henry Farnham, not guilty of theft," she said. "On the second count of vandalizing government property, we find the defendant guilty as charged."

5

Passing Sentence

Henry Farnham smiled with relief when he heard the jury's verdict. But after a brief conversation with Fran Jerome, the smile faded. Every guilty verdict must be followed by a sentence. Like almost all judges, Reilly took that task seriously. What was the proper punishment? Many Americans thought the answer to crime was to get tough. Some of his own friends often urged him to 'lock 'em up and throw away the key."

Is prison the best way to punish criminals? Those who say "yes" believe that the fear of going to prison prevents crime. But does this deterrent effect actually work? Criminal justice experts aren't sure. Perhaps the fear of arrest and imprisonment keeps the average person from committing a crime. But Judge Reilly had learned that most streetwise criminals never expected to be caught. They seldom worried about going to prison.

Prison sentences also seem to satisfy the age-old desire for justice. But even though most people believe society should punish those who break its laws, the use of prison sentences creates additional problems. For example, prisons are expensive to build and maintain. Every year of prison time costs U.S. taxpayers around $18,000 per inmate. It's cheaper to send people to college than to send them to prison.

Another reason for locking up criminals is based on the idea of

*Sentencing is perhaps the most difficult part of a judge's job,
and the toughest sentence is one of death. This Louisiana inmate
is on death row.*

rehabilitation. In theory, prison should help inmates finish their schooling and learn useful skills. Prison counselors are supposed to help convicts develop positive attitudes about themselves, so that when they leave prison they will be better able to find good jobs and build new lives.

The reality was very different, Reilly knew. Even though cruel and unusual punishments have been outlawed, prisoners must endure boredom, fear, and isolation. There aren't enough prison guards to keep the stronger inmates from taking advantage of the weak. Facilities for taking classes or learning new job skills are often nonexistent. And instead of being rehabilitated, seven out of ten convicts commit new crimes after they're released.

All this was in Judge Reilly's mind as he thanked the jury for its work. Then he ordered Farnham to return to court in two weeks for sentencing. Later that day he'd ask Peggy Waldorf to prepare a probation report. He needed more information before deciding on a sentence.

All Prisons Aren't The Same

"Duncan, you're not eating your dinner. Is anything wrong?" Roberta Reilly looked both concerned and annoyed.

Reilly looked up, aware that his mind had been far away. Well, ten miles anyway—at the courthouse. He explained that he'd been thinking over his sentencing options for Henry Farnham.

"Let's assume that an offender's crime deserves a year or two in prison," he said. "The choices don't end there. It's also my job to choose the prison best fitted to the offender and the crime."

Ten-year-old Jimmy had been listening in on this adult conversation. "Aren't all prisons about the same?" he asked.

Reilly glanced at his son. "Out of about 30,000 federal prisoners, only the most dangerous ones are sent to maximum security prisons," he said. "That's where they have the stone walls and massive blocks of cells that you see in the movies."

"So, how do you decide on the right place to send someone?" Jimmy asked.

"First, I have to consider the crime," Reilly told him. "Less serious crimes are called misdemeanors. If you trespassed on federal property, you'd be guilty of a misdemeanor. The maximum sentence for a misdemeanor is a year in jail. But let's say you also stole a computer. Now you've committed a felony. The sentence would be at least a year and a day in prison. Did you assault a guard while you were stealing the computer? Adding violence to the crime could earn you a much longer sentence."

"What about those 'country-club prisons' we read about in the newspapers?" Mrs. Reilly asked.

"The proper name is 'correctional institution'," Reilly laughed. "The one I visited didn't look much like a country club, believe me. The inmates were housed in old wooden buildings and the place was surrounded by a high electric fence. But there was a gym, a ball field, and a crafts shop. The staff taught job skills and held group counseling sessions. Some prisoners earned weekend 'furloughs' that let them visit their families."

"What if *I* stole that computer?" Jimmy asked. "Would I be put in prison with all the other criminals?"

Reilly smiled and squeezed his son's shoulder. "At your age, you'd probably be released to the custody of your parents," he said. "Your mother and I would be responsible for making sure you didn't steal again. If you were older, you might be sent to a work camp or a reformatory for juvenile delinquents. The camps emphasize rehabilitation, not punishment. The idea is to turn young people around so they don't become career criminals."

Alternatives To Prison

When he read about the cruelty of prison life, Judge Reilly remembered a Supreme Court ruling. In *Rhodes v. Chapman* the court had said, "The Constitution does not mandate comfortable prisons...To the extent that prison conditions are restrictive, even harsh, they are part of the penalty that criminal offenders pay for their offenses against society."

"Even so," Reilly thought, "prison isn't always the best way to punish a nonviolent criminal. What if I don't send Farnham to prison? What are my options?"

One was to send the young man to a residential treatment program where, during the day, Farnham would go out to a regular job. When he wasn't working, he'd be confined to the center's guarded building. If his reading and math skills were poor, he'd be sent to class to improve them. Counselors would teach him ways of controlling his anger. The record showed that this program worked. The average stay at the facility was only four to five months, compared to 14 months in a regular prison.

Violence continues to plague cities, much of it caused by drug wars and gang conflicts. Many criminal cases are resolved by plea bargaining, meaning relatively few violent criminals are ever punished by imprisonment.

Judge Reilly had visited the nearest residential treatment program. Inmates were dressed in regular clothes and moved freely about the building. They showed none of the bottled-up rage he'd seen during his prison visits. A young woman had surprised him with her positive comments about the facility.

"I know it was stupid for me to take some money from the bank," she said. "But since I had to serve time anyway, I'm glad you sent me here. I've learned some new computer skills and me and my kids haven't had to go on welfare. You won't see me in your court again."

Reilly had also read about experiments with a system of house arrest where nonviolent prisoners wore tiny radio transmitters locked to their legs. A monitoring station kept track of where they were at all times. If they left home outside of working hours, the station notified the police to pick them up. The system saved the taxpayers money and allowed the prisoners to live an almost normal home life. Very few of them committed new crimes after they were released.

"I don't think I'm a soft-hearted judge," Reilly confided to his wife. "But except for the really vicious crimes, I believe more in rehabilitation than I do in punishment. If I can keep defendants out of prison without endangering the public, I'll do it. I hope Henry Farnham receives a favorable probation report."

The Sentencing

That night, Reilly tried to explain the difference between probation and parole to his son. Probation, he said, meant that convicted defendants were set free with the threat of prison sentences still hanging over their heads. They had to report to their probation officer regularly. Parole meant prisoners were released after serving only part of their sentences. With time off for good behavior, an inmate might serve only two or three years of a five-year sentence.

The right to grant or deny parole for federal prisoners belongs to the U.S. Parole Commission. The commission only grants paroles when it is sure that doing so is in the public interest. Even the most hardened prisoners can apply for parole, but they are often turned down.

The Debate Over
The Death Penalty

As crime rates rise the public demands tougher law enforcement and more severe penalties for convicted criminals. Capital punishment—the death sentence—is the most severe punishment of all. With the murder rate in the U.S. nearing 20,000 victims a year, the demand for tougher law enforcement has grown stronger than ever. In a 1976 ruling, a divided Supreme Court said that the death penalty was constitutional as long as the states administered it fairly. Despite this, and despite the fact that over 2,000 convicts are currently on death row, very few executions take place. Who's right and who's wrong? In the following debate, the Pro side supports capital punishment and the Con side argues against it.

Pro

1. Execution is the only sure way to keep convicted killers from killing again. Even in prison, they are still a threat to the guards who supervise them.

2. The death penalty is a strong deterrent to potential murderers. It would be an even greater deterrent if it were applied swiftly and surely whenever a death sentence is passed on a convicted murderer.

Con

1. Life imprisonment without parole keeps convicted killers off the streets without placing society in the degrading role of executioner.

2. No firm evidence supports the theory that the death penalty deters potential murderers. The murder rate in the 39 states that have capital punishment is just as high as it is in the 11 states that do not execute murderers.

The Debate Over The Death Penalty

3. Society has a right to punish those responsible for taking the lives of innocent people. Execution is a logical punishment for the crime of taking another person's life.

3. Civilized societies do not need to practice barbaric "eye-for-an-eye" justice. Life sentences without parole are more than adequate punishment for the crime of murder.

4. The states do not apply the death penalty carelessly. Condemned prisoners are allowed to file appeals that last for years. Although there are over 2,000 prisoners on death row, less than one percent are executed each year.

4. The death penalty falls most often on members of racial minorities and the poor. The long appeals process has again and again confirmed the fact that the courts are not "blind" when it comes to handing down death sentences.

5. Swift application of the death penalty would save the taxpayers the cost of feeding and housing murderers who otherwise spend many years in prison.

5. The expense of legal fees and court time, plus the extra costs of keeping prisoners on death row more than equal the costs of a life sentence.

Both parole and probation were judgment calls, Reilly knew. That was why Probation Officer Peggy Waldorf was looking into Farnham's background. Waldorf interviewed everyone connected with the case, including Farnham. Was he truly sorry for what he had done? Had he learned his lesson?

Farnham said that the night he'd spent in jail after his arrest was enough to last him a lifetime. He had already enrolled in a government training program to learn new job skills. At the moment, however, he was still out of a job. His boss fired him the day he came back to work after he had been arrested.

The probation officer called around and found a company that was willing to hire him. The owner knew from experience that most probationers were excellent workers. Their fear of prison tended to keep their minds on their work.

Finally, there was the problem of Farnham's temper. Waldorf sent him to a public mental health center. Farnham argued that he didn't need to see a "shrink," but he kept the appointment. To his surprise, he found it easy to talk to the sympathetic young counselor. The weekly sessions he attended taught him better ways of expressing his feelings.

With the study complete, Waldorf sent her report to Judge Reilly. The judge smiled as he read, "I recommend probation for Henry Farnham. No useful purpose would be served by sending him to prison."

When Farnham returned to court, Judge Reilly ordered him to pay for the damage he'd caused, then put him on probation for two years. During that time, he said, the young man must continue in counseling. He also sentenced him to put in 200 hours of community service with the U.S. Forest Service.

"If you violate your probation," Reilly warned, "you will be picked up and sent to prison for one year."

6

Hearing A Civil Case

Roberta Reilly showed the tattered remains of a silk blouse to her husband. "I paid over $100 for that blouse and the dry cleaners won't admit they made a mistake," she complained. "I'm thinking of filing suit in small claims court."

Judge Reilly looked at the blouse with a critical eye. This wasn't a criminal case, he thought. No federal or state law had been broken. If it went to court it would be a civil case, one in which the injured party sued to recover damages.

"Well, do I have a case?" Mrs. Reilly demanded.

"You certainly have suffered an injury," Reilly agreed. "That's the first test in a civil suit. Was the dry cleaners liable for the damage to your blouse? That's the second test."

"I talked to the owner when I took the blouse in," Mrs. Reilly said. "Gary promised to give it special care."

Reilly nodded. "Your case seems to meet both tests," he said. "Because the damages are less than $2,000, you can file in small claims court."

Mrs. Reilly filed her suit for $125 in the state's Small Claims Court the next day. In the federal court system, she knew, only the Federal Tax Court allows small claims. The filing fee was just $6. That was typical of the entire process. With no lawyers and no jury,

In American law, every witness may be cross-examined to challenge their testimony. In criminal trials, this is known as the right to "confront one's accuser."

everything was simplified. When the case came to trial, a judge would hear the case without a jury.

The court notified Gary Simon that she had filed suit. When the trial date arrived, Mrs. Reilly's case was only one of many on the court's calendar. One case involved a dog bite, another a faulty car repair. Another man was suing his neighbor because the neighbor's tree had fallen on his car.

When Mrs. Reilly's case was called, she showed the torn blouse to the court. Next she showed the judge the bill of sale to prove the value of the blouse. Finally, she produced the receipt on which Simon had written, "Special handling required."

Then it was the dry cleaners' turn. Simon claimed that the blouse had been in poor shape when she gave it to him. "I'm no magician," he said. "I can't make clothes look like new."

The judge asked a few questions before telling them to expect her decision in the mail. A week later, Mrs. Reilly received a letter from the court. The judge had awarded her the full $125 plus the court costs. Two days later, she received a check from Simon for the full amount.

That night, an elated Roberta Reilly showed the check to her husband. Judge Reilly told her that she was lucky. Speedy action in a civil case was unusual. Some of the complex civil cases that came to his district court took months to resolve.

First Steps In A Civil Case

Judge Reilly was studying papers that described a civil suit he would soon be hearing. The case had been filed three years ago and was just now coming to trial. "Americans are sure quick to sue each other when they think they've been injured," he thought. In fact, federal district courts stagger under an overload of almost 240,000 civil cases every year.

The Constitution defines what civil cases can be filed in federal court. Federal judges hear cases "arising under this Constitution, the laws of the United States, and treaties made under their authority." Suits filed by one state against another and suits filed by a citizen of one state against a citizen of another state also go to the federal courts. Rare cases that involve foreign diplomats are also handled by federal courts.

Reilly remembered some of the cases in which he'd been involved. An engineer had sued a major department store chain, claiming that the company was selling a tool he'd invented. A civil rights group had asked the court to protect the voting rights of the city's minority population. An old woman had sued to recover her life savings that were lost in a mail fraud scheme. A trucking company had asked for relief from a ruling by the Interstate Commerce Commission. The company claimed the federal agency's ruling was forcing it to operate at a loss.

Each case began when lawyers for the *plaintiff* (the person bringing the suit) filed papers in district court. The plaintiff first had to prove that the case belonged in the federal courts. If the court accepted the case, the plaintiff then served a summons on the defendant. The summons notified the defendant that the suit has been filed and must be answered.

Just filing a suit can often bring about a settlement. Long court trials are expensive for both sides, no matter who wins. Reilly remembered a tactic used by a lumber company against a group called "Save the Trees." The environmental group had filed suit to stop the company from logging a nearby forest. At the same time, Save the Trees had asked for and been granted a temporary injunction. The court order stopped the logging operation until the case could be heard. Without injunctions, plaintiffs might be subjected to further harm while waiting for their cases to come to trial.

The lumber company struck back with a countersuit that claimed its operations were being unfairly damaged by Save the Trees. Faced with the countersuit, Save the Trees withdrew its own suit. The lumber company could afford a long trial, but Save the Trees couldn't.

The Pretrail Maneuvers

At first glance, the case of *Baker v. Paradox Appliances* seemed simple enough. Marina Baker (the plaintiff) had been badly scalded when a Paradox coffee pot exploded in her kitchen. She was suing Paradox (the defendant) for $1 million. The money, her suit said, was fair compensation for her injuries, emotional suffering, and lost work time. The suit was filed in a federal court because Paradox had its headquarters in an eastern state.

Baker's personal injury suit was known as a *tort* action. In a tort, the plaintiff asks for compensation for damages caused by the defendant. In a second type of civil suit, the plaintiff claims that the defendant has broken a written or oral *contract*. If Paradox had failed to deliver a shipment of coffee pots, its customers could have filed for damages under contract law. In a third type of suit, the plaintiff claims to have been injured by an unconstitutional or illegal act of a government body. Suits filed to protect voting rights, to integrate schools, and to seek new trials for prisoners fall into this category.

In their reply to Baker, the Paradox lawyers had asked Reilly to dismiss the suit. They claimed that the coffee pot was perfectly safe when

Filing A Suit
In Small Claims Court

Small claims court lets people obtain a quick and impartial decision in a legal conflict. Did the landlord refuse to return your security deposit? Was your car damaged by a falling city power line? Did your neighbor's cat shred your lawn chair? Not every problem, however, can be taken to small claims court. Before filing a claim, you should answer the following questions:

Question	Discussion
Do you have a case?	You cannot collect damages unless (1) you have suffered a loss, and (2) the person or company you are suing is legally liable.
How large is your claim?	Each state sets a maximum amount that you can recover in small claims court—usually $2,000. If your loss is greater than that, you must either file in a higher court or give up your rights to anything over the maximum amount allowed.
Has time run out on your claim?	Statutes of Limitations set time limits for recovering damages. The typical limit is one year. If you wait too long, you may be denied the right to file your claim.

Filing A Suit
In Small Claims Court

Where do you file your claim?

If you and the defendant both live in the same city or country, file your suit locally. If defendant lives in another state, you'll have to file in that state.

Whom can you sue?

You can file a claim against almost anyone or any group—a person, a partnership, a corporation, or a government agency. When filing a claim against a business, you must sue its owner or owners. The names you need can be obtained from the county clerk in the county where the company does business.

Did you try to settle the dispute?

Most small claims courts expect you to make an effort to settle your claim before you file suit. A compromise settlement that avoids a court date saves time, money and stress.

Do you have a good chance of collecting?

Winning a court judgment is a hollow victory if the defendant is broke. You can't collect from someone who doesn't have any money or a business that is bankrupt.

used properly. The plaintiff's lawyers submitted evidence showing that nine other Paradox coffee pots had exploded during the past year. With that in mind, Reilly had asked both sides to begin the *discovery* process.

During discovery, the two sides exchanged information. Much of the information was collected from witnesses through *depositions*. In one deposition, a Paradox engineer testified under oath about the safety features designed into the coffee pot. In another, Baker's doctor described her injuries and the treatment she received. The opposing attorneys were present at each deposition and had the right to question the witnesses. A court reporter was hired to record the testimony and to prepare the printed depositions.

After discovery was completed, Judge Reilly called a pretrial conference. During this informal meeting he encouraged the two sides to settle the case. The Paradox lawyers offered a $100,000 settlement, but Baker's attorneys turned it down. Reilly knew they were hoping to win a much larger award from a trial jury. Since the attorneys were working for a percentage of Baker's award, a smaller settlement also meant a smaller fee.

When the settlement offer failed, Reilly set a trial date. The judge could have heard the case without a jury if both sides had agreed. Baker's lawyers, however, asked for a jury trial. They felt certain that a jury would be more sympathetic to their badly scarred client.

The Civil Trial

The trial of *Baker v. Paradox* began with the selection of a six-person jury. Judge Reilly told the jury that the rules of proof differed in a civil case. "In this case," he said, "you can find for the plaintiff even though her case has not been proved beyond reasonable doubt. You must find for whichever side presents the strongest case, based on the evidence."

The trial began with opening statements. Baker's lawyer described the accident in vivid detail. When he pointed to his client, Reilly noticed that Baker's make-up emphasized her scars. For his part, the Paradox lawyer said that Baker must have misused the coffee pot. He ended by telling the jury that "suits such as this drive up prices for all consumers." That comment brought a strong objection from his opponent. Reilly upheld the objection and instructed the jury to disregard the comment.

Baker's lawyer then presented his case. It was his job to prove that Paradox was liable for the accident. His witnesses testified that Mrs. Baker was a careful woman. She had never had a similar accident. Several witnesses also testified about their own problems with Paradox appliances.

The defendant's lawyer tore into the plaintiff's witnesses during cross-examination. Mrs. Baker, a neighbor admitted, was a heavy sleeper who was often half-asleep when she made her morning coffee. In fact, she'd bought the new coffee pot after ruining an old one by letting it boil dry. The jury now realized that the case had two sides.

When the plaintiff's lawyer rested his case, the Paradox lawyer asked Judge Reilly to dismiss the suit for lack of evidence. Reilly ruled against him. Unruffled, he then presented his own case. His key witness was an electrical engineer who testified that the coffee pot was safely designed. On cross-examination, the engineer admitted that there was a very small chance it could explode—if it were used improperly.

After the closing arguments, Reilly instructed the jurors in the issues to be decided, and in the rules of law that applied to this case. If the case had clearly favored one side or the other, he could have directed the jury to vote for that side.

In the jury room, the six men and women reviewed the testimony. They examined the ruined coffee pot and read the instruction sheet aloud. The pictures of Mrs. Baker's injuries and the scars she retained decided the jurors in her favor. Because they agreed that her carelessness may have been a factor in the accident, however, they reduced her $1 million claim to $250,000.

Judge Reilly was satisfied with the 6-0 verdict. If the jury had ignored the weight of the evidence, he could have ordered a new trial. If the award had been too high, he could have reduced it. In this case, he did neither. He instructed Paradox to pay the $250,000 plus court costs, and recessed the court.

7

Filing An Appeal

Judge Reilly frowned and slammed the phone down. He'd just been told that Congressman Scopolus was appealing his conviction under the federal election laws. Reilly wasn't surprised, but he was annoyed. What if the appeals court reversed the decision? Would that mean that he had done a poor job of conducting the original trial?

"Hold on," Reilly told himself. "You did your best in the Scopolus trial. If an appellate court reverses you, it means only that the appeals judges are doing their jobs. The courts of appeals exist to protect individual rights. After all, judges and juries do make mistakes."

If a trial court is found to be in error, the appeals court provides a means of correcting it. The roots of the process are firmly anchored in our history. As far back as the 1300s, English defendants had won the right to appeal their convictions to the King's Bench. Knowing that a higher court could review their decisions kept the lower courts honest and careful.

Reilly visualized the route that the congressman's appeal would take. First it would go to the nearest U.S. Court of Appeals. There is one court of appeals in each of the nation's 12 judicial districts. A separate appeals court handles special cases involving patents, customs, and claims against the federal government. Some courts of appeals have as few as six judges assigned to them, while the busier courts have as many as 28.

Over 30,000 cases a year flood into the appeals courts. More than two-thirds are civil cases, although criminal cases tend to attract more attention. Most cases are heard by three-judge panels. The decision to deny or uphold an appeal doesn't have to be unanimous. Many appeals are decided on votes of 2-1.

The losers in the courts of appeals have one final chance. Reilly guessed that, if necessary, Scopolus would pursue his appeal all the way to the U.S. Supreme Court. The same route is open to defendants and plaintiffs who lose on appeal in a state supreme court. Filing an appeal with the Supreme Court, however, doesn't guarantee that the case will be heard. The nation's highest court has time to review only the most important cases. Of every 100 cases that are appealed to the Supreme Court, only four are accepted for review. The decision of the lower court is allowed to stand in the other 96.

The Appeal

As a district court judge, Duncan Reilly studied the actions of the appeals courts with great care. He knew that only one case in eight is appealed. Of those that do reach the courts of appeals, only one in ten is reversed. Unless he'd been lazy, careless, or dictatorial in his handling of the Scopolus case, he shouldn't have to worry about being overruled on appeal.

In a typical reversal, the appeals court throws out some of the evidence used in the case. Judge Reilly remembered a trial that had been decided by a bag of cocaine the police found in the defendant's car. He had allowed the cocaine to be entered as evidence, but the appeals court ruled that it was obtained by an illegal search. Such "tainted" evidence cannot be used in court. The defendant was given a new trial, and convicted again. Reilly had enjoyed that small victory.

The appeals courts sometimes disagree with the lower courts without reversing them. Some decisions are either narrowed or broadened. The appeals judges issue these opinions in the form of *dicta*. District judges are expected to study them and to use them as guidance in future cases. At other times, the appeals judges vacate only part of a decision. That's more likely to happen in a civil case. When a district court is given one of these partial reversals, it has to retry that part of

The most powerful court in America, the United States Supreme Court of 1990. Front row (left to right): Thurgood Marshall, William Brennan, Chief Justice William Rehnquist, Byron White and Harry Blackmun. Back row: Antonin Scalia, John Paul Stevens, Sandra Day O'Connor and Anthony Kennedy.

the case that has been vacated.

The appeals process itself is governed by strict rules. The prosecution cannot appeal a "guilty" verdict in a criminal case. On the other side, convicted defendants cannot appeal the facts in a case. Their appeals must be based on points of law. Many cases are appealed because the losers believe that a judge's errors denied them a fair trial. Even though Henry Farnham's trial had been a simple one, for example, Judge Reilly had been required to make dozens of decisions. Had he unknowingly favored the prosecution during the arraignment? Had he unfairly denied a defense motion to restrict the post office clerk's testimony? Had he given incorrect instructions to the jury?

Well, Henry Farnham wasn't going to appeal. That young man was overjoyed with the verdict and the sentence he'd received.

The Decision-Making Process

Judge Reilly enjoyed his work on the district court, but he was also an ambitious man. If he made a name for himself as a solid, hard-working judge, he could be appointed to the appeals court.

The appeals court was on his mind when he met Wilson McKeever for lunch. Reilly's old law school professor was now sitting on the Fifth District Court of Appeals. The two friends ate barbecued shrimp and chatted about their families. When Reilly asked about the appeals court, Judge McKeever's eyes lit up. "I'm working harder than ever," he said, "but the appeals court gives me a chance to explore the deeper meaning of the law. If someone appeals that new tax law, I may have the pleasure of declaring some part of it unconstitutional."

Then he paused for a moment and thought about what he'd just said. "No—whatever my personal opinions are, I must be objective. The appeals court examines every case in the light of earlier cases, the precedents we all studied in law school. But I also look at each case on its own merits. We don't accept a case on appeal unless valid points of law or judicial error are involved."

"How heavy is your caseload?" Reilly asked.

"Our work cycle is different than yours," McKeever replied. He explained that his panel of three judges began a cycle by hearing about 30 cases in a week's session. They prepared for these court ses-

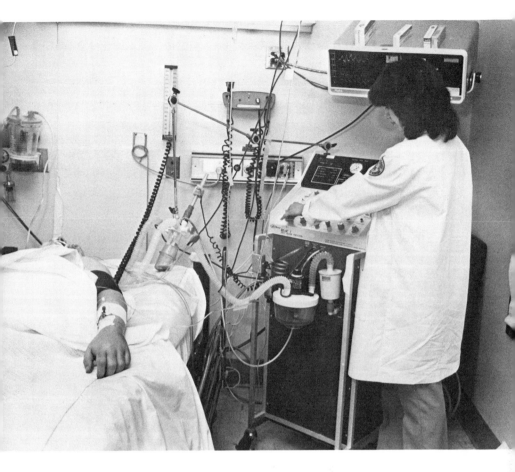

Many legal experts believe the 1990s will see a rise in cases concerning the "right to die"—and the U.S. Supreme Court will be asked to clear up the many state rulings that have blurred this sensitive issue.

sions by reading the briefs prepared by the attorneys. The oral arguments in each case were limited to about an hour. After listening to the attorneys, the judges often tried to clarify the arguments by asking pointed questions.

Afterward, the judges spent three weeks in their chambers discussing their decisions and writing their opinions. "We argue a lot," McKeever said with a smile. "But decisions emerge out of all that smoke and fire. One of the judges on the majority side is assigned to write the opinion. The judge who's outvoted can write a minority opinion if he or she feels strongly that the majority side has erred."

Youthful offenders are sent to juvenile courts where judges hear their cases informally and without a jury. The goal here is to rehabilitate young people before they commit more serious crimes. Unfortunately, the juvenile courts have not always provided youthful offenders with the rights that are routinely guaranteed to adults. Juveniles, for example, are sometimes given longer sentences than adults convicted of the same offense. Much of that unfairness changed in 1967, when the case of In re Gault reached the Supreme Court, described below.

The Case	Description
The offense	Gerald Gault was 15 when a neighbor accused him of making a "lewd and offensive" phone call. The Arizona youth was on probation at the time for an earlier offense.
The arrest	Gerald's parents were not at home when he was arrested by the police. They were not notifed that he had been picked up.
Court action	The juvenile court hearing was held the next day. Gerald was not represented by a lawyer nor was he allowed to confront the neighbor who filed the charges. He was not advised of his right to remain

silent. The judge sentenced Gerald to be held in the state reformatory until age 21—a six year sentence.

The appeal

Arizona law did not permit the filing of an appeal in a juvenile case. Gerald's parents turned to the federal courts. Their lawyer argued that the boy's rights under the due process clause of the 14th Amendment had been violated. The Supreme Court agreed to review the case.

The decision

The Supreme Court ruled that Gerald's rights had been violated. The decision listed four constitutional guarantees that could not be overlooked: (1) Juveniles and their parents or guardians must be given written notice of all charges. (2) Juveniles have the right to be represented by a lawyer. If they cannot afford a lawyer, the state must provide one. (3) Juveniles (and their lawyers) have the right to confront witnesses and to cross-examine them. (4) Juveniles must be advised of their right to remain silent.

"I've seen opinions that ran only a few lines," Reilly said. "Others go on for a hundred pages or more."

"We're aiming at well-written opinions," McKeever said. "That's why all of us read the drafts and suggest changes. If our opinions are good enough, they can be used as guides for making decisions in the lower courts."

"And if a losing appellant thinks you goofed, you can be sure the case will be appealed to the Supreme Court," Reilly laughed.

◊ The Court Of Last Resort

Every judge makes national policy to some degree, Judge Reilly knew. If I make a decision and it stands on appeal, other judges may use that decision as a precedent. But only the United States Supreme Court serves as the ultimate national policymaker.

Reilly had toured the Supreme Court building while he was in Washington for his confirmation hearings. The beautiful marble building, five stories tall, covers an entire block. The words "Equal Justice Under Law" are carved above the entrance. The courtroom where the nine justices hear cases is elegantly paneled in wood. At the beginning of a court session, a marshal calls for order. Then the nine justices enter through red velvet drapes to take their seats behind the bench. A guide told Reilly that about 4,000 cases are appealed to the high court each year. The justices, however, order the lower courts to forward case records for only 250 of them or less. The Supreme Court's refusal to hear the other cases leaves intact the decisions issued by the lower courts. Of the 250 cases the opposing lawyers argue before the court, the justices issue written opinions in only 150. The others are reported with a note that the case has been either "affirmed" or "reversed."

In this same courtroom, Reilly knew, justices had arrived at decisions that shaped the nation's way of life. If a law or government action violated the Constitution, the Supreme Court could declare it unconstitutional. That power did more than make the court an equal branch of government. It cast the court in the role of guardian of individual rights and freedoms.

Like many Americans, Reilly had mixed feelings about the role played by the courts. He tended to favor those courts that practiced *judicial restraint*. This approach produces courts that are reluctant to overrule established decisions. It's up to Congress and the president to write and execute new laws, these courts say. But there was also a place for *judicial activism*, Reilly knew. Activist courts attacked social issues that the other two branches ignored. It was judicial activists who greatly expanded the nation's civil rights protections during the 1960s.

Sitting on the Supreme Court must give a judge an awesome sense of power, Reilly concluded. When the high court makes a decision, there's no other court to hear an appeal. As a citizen you have only two choices. You can accept the decision, or you can begin a campaign to amend the Constitution.

8

The Court System Isn't Perfect

J udge Reilly liked Vic Armstrong at once. He'd worried about how it would look for a district judge to appear on a television talk show, but the host quickly put him at ease.

"You can help the public understand the importance of the courts by speaking out," Armstrong assured him. When Fran Jerome walked onto the set, Reilly felt even better. The public defender was outspoken enough to carry the program all by herself.

A producer counted down the seconds to air time and the cameras zoomed in on the small set. Armstrong's expression became stern and his voice deepened. "Welcome to *Public Interest*," he said. "Today we're going to take a hard look at the problems of the American judicial system."

"Let's start with the issue of legal costs," the host continued. "The average person is being priced out of the courts. Let's say a working man makes $7 or $8 an hour. He's being sued because an old woman tripped over a garden hose he left lying on the sidewalk. He needs an attorney, but lawyers bill their services at over $100 an hour. Even if he wins the case, the working guy gets stuck with a legal bill equal to a year's salary."

Fran Jerome jumped on the question. "In criminal cases, the poor can ask for a public defender," she said. "In civil suits, they have to depend on volunteer legal aid clinics. That works as long as the federal and state governments support these clinics. But budgets are being cut back and the clinics are overwhelmed with clients. The poor and elderly are being victimized because no one's protecting their rights."

Reilly spoke up to defend his old profession. "I think it's more a question of teaching people how to use the system," he said. "The people who file suit in small claims court can argue their own cases. Court costs are minimal and justice is quick. As for the working guy, he could look around for a lawyer who's willing to do *pro bono* work. Many lawyers volunteer some of their time to work without pay for the public good."

"Personal injury lawyers take up to one-half of a plaintiff's settlement," Armstrong cut in. "Are they doing *pro bono* work?"

"Call them what they are: 'ambulance-chasers'," Jerome said scornfully.

Both of them looked at Reilly. He held up his hands in mock surrender. "Don't look at me," he said. "Judges aren't part of the problem. Our courts are open to everyone, rich or poor. Besides, I make less money than almost all of the lawyers who appear in my courtroom."

Do The Courts Move Too Slowly?

Vic Armstrong shook his head. "You say that judges aren't part of the problem, Judge Reilly. But cases that involve large sums of money or long prison sentences take months to come to trial. Those that do make it into court are often wrapped up in a few minutes. On the other hand, there's one case in district court that involves a large corporation and an army of expensive lawyers. That case has been taking up court time for over a year. What's going on?"

"You've brought up two separate issues," Reilly said. "First, there's the problem of caseload. We have more cases waiting to be heard than we have courtrooms and judges to hear them. Second, to add to the problem, attorneys use delaying tactics whenever they think it will help their clients."

"Taxpayers want justice to be swift, but they don't want to pay the taxes needed to build more courtrooms," Reilly said. "I'm all for getting tough with drug dealers, for example. But we can't lock them up

One of the most controversial judicial rulings of recent times was
Roe v. Wade, *the 1973 decision that legalized abortion. These
anti-abortion protestors are picketing in front of the U.S. Supreme Court.*

until they've had their day in court."

"No one wants higher taxes," Armstrong agreed. "But aren't we getting assembly-line justice?"

"The courts are like a busy doctor's office," Reilly said. "Much of the work takes place behind the scenes. The judge has already held a preliminary hearing and conferred with the lawyers. Perhaps a plea bargain has been arranged. Nine out of ten defendants plead guilty, so their courtroom appearances are just a formality. If defendants feel shortchanged, they have plenty of chances to ask the judge to explain their rights."

Fran Jerome had her own ideas about speeding up the court system. "Some of Judge Reilly's fellow judges are part of the problem," she said. "I know judges who don't start work until 10 o'clock, then they're on the golf course four hours later. There are others who take months to write their decisions in even the simplest civil suits. We should give judges heavier caseloads and throw out cases that haven't come to trial within six months."

"Forcing the courts to meet artificial deadlines doesn't work," countered Reilly. "The states that have tried it backed off quickly. Let's be efficient, by all means, but not at the expense of our constitutional rights."

Do The Courts Overstep Their Authority?

"I think we all agree that society depends on the courts to punish the guilty," Armstrong said to the camera. "But are the courts doing their job? Let me show you some statistics gathered from the criminal courts of New York City."

A graphic appeared on the monitor in front of them.

Of every 100 felonies committed:

- only 20 suspects are arrested; the other 80 go free.

- 8 of the 20 suspects are dismissed or jump bail.

- Of the 12 who go to trial, 1 is acquitted, 9 plead guilty to a lesser charge, and 2 are convicted on the original charges.

- Of these 11 convicted felons, 5 go to prison; the other 6 receive probation.

"Those numbers are scary," Reilly said. "But statistics can be misleading. Let's assume that 10 of those suspects were repeat offenders and 10 were first offenders. As a rule we lock up eight of the ex-cons, but only two of the first offenders."

"I'm with the judge on this one," Jerome said. "I want judges to fit the punishment to the crime. Lock up the murderers and rapists and

The Qualities That Make A Good Judge

The American judicial system is no better than the men and women who serve as its judges. Legal experts who have studied the work of outstanding judges have found that they share the following six personal and professional qualities.

The Quality	Why Is It Important?
1. Judges must be neutral.	Judges must not show favoritism toward either plaintiffs or defendants. They must interpret the law in such a way that everyone who enters their courtrooms is judged fairly.
2. Judges must know the law.	Good judges must have a sound training in the law and must have practiced as attorneys. They must constantly update their knowledge of the law, knowing that it is affected by higher court decisions and acts of the other two branches of government.
3. Judges must think, speak, and write clearly.	The ability to communicate clearly and forcefully is a vital skill for judges. Judges must follow complex arguments, issue clear rulings, instruct juries properly, and write logical, well-reasoned opinions.

The Qualities That Make A Good Judge

4. Judges must have personal integrity.

Every judge comes under political and economic pressures, but good judges must ignore outside influences. They must interpret the law and manage their courtrooms according to high moral and ethical standards.

5. Judges must have a judicial temperament.

Judges must remain calm and even-tempered even when tensions run high in their courtrooms. They must be courteous; if challenged, they must be stern without being dictatorial.

6. Judges must be in good health.

Judges who are in poor health or who are dependent upon drugs or alcohol cannot work effectively. Similarly, judges with severe emotional problems cannot bring the necessary judgment and intellect to their courtrooms.

big-time drug dealers. But show mercy when you're sentencing people who can still turn their lives around."

Reilly was thinking about the Sentencing Act of 1987. Like many federal judges, he was upset by the exact guidelines Congress had written into the law. What's the use of putting on my robes, he thought, if I'm not free to hand down sentences tailored to each individual case?

Before Reilly could speak, Armstrong hit on a new topic. "Many people say the courts have gone beyond interpreting the law," the host said. "They charge that judges are making law."

"Changing times require new interpretations of the law," Reilly said patiently. "A century ago judges were expected to stick to the letter of the law. As a result many social ills went unaddressed. Today's judges are much more likely to interpret the law in light of changing social conditions."

Armstrong looked horrified. "Are you saying that the law is whatever a judge says it is?" he asked.

"Sure, it looks as though a Supreme Court majority can rewrite the law," Reilly said. "But even the high court has limits. Judges can't make decisions until someone files suit or until a suspect is indicted. Judges can't pass new laws. Most importantly, judges think long and hard before they overturn an act of the legislature. Just because a law is bad or foolish doesn't make it unconstitutional."

Are The Courts Doing Anything Right?

After the talk show ended, Judge Reilly went for a walk in a nearby park. He felt frustrated. Time had run out before he could talk about the positive side of the court system.

Reilly thought of the progress made in civil rights. The courts had been ten years ahead of Congress in moving against segregated schools. Later, when school districts dragged their feet, federal judges set up busing plans to end segregation.

Women and minorities were moving into better jobs because of court-ordered hiring plans. The influence of the courts was also being felt in state and national politics. With every vote counting equally, more women and minorities were being elected in greater numbers.

The successes in civil rights, Reilly knew, didn't cancel all the criticisms. How would he reform the judicial system? First, paying off political debts with court appointments put too many ill-prepared judges on the federal bench. But even competent judges can grow old and tired in a lifetime job. He believed Congress should set up a blue-ribbon review panel. If problem judges didn't improve, the panel would recommend their removal.

Next, the system needed to be streamlined. The courts were clogged with civil cases that could easily be handled by trained arbitrators. Armed with common sense and a little legal training, these officials could hold hearings in neighborhood justice centers. Sure, it's every citizen's right to sue, but the higher courts should be saved for the more important cases.

Finally, Reilly believed in making the courts more accessible. Write documents in plain English, and make sure every judge puts in a full day's work. Guarantee every plaintiff and every defendant the services of a competent attorney. Being rich shouldn't give anyone an advantage in the courtroom.

A glance at his watch sent Reilly hurrying back to the courthouse. Half an hour later he opened a hearing on a petition from a prisoners' rights group. Their lawyer asked him to close down the county jail, now bulging at 400 prisoners over capacity. It promised to be a tough call. If he granted the injunction, the sheriff would probably have to release some of the prisoners.

But that's not the issue, Reilly decided. Is the over-crowded jail a threat to the prisoners' health and safety? If it is, I must issue the injunction.

With that thought in mind, Judge Reilly rapped the bench with his gavel. He told the lawyers he would inspect the jail before he made his decision. "I don't like the idea of releasing prisoners early," he said, "but the law must be enforced fairly."

Glossary

ADMINISTRATIVE LAW. Rulings issued by federal agencies that have the force of law.

ARRAIGNMENT. The stage in the criminal justice process when suspects appear before a judge to hear the charges filed against them and to enter their pleas of guilty or not guilty.

BAIL. Money or personal property left on deposit with the court to guarantee the return of a defendant for trial. Nonviolent defendants are often released with a promise to return.

BAR EXAM. The test which lawyers must pass before they are permitted to practice law in any given state.

COMMON LAW. The body of law that gains its authority from custom and earlier court decisions.

CONSTITUTIONAL LAW. The body of law based on the U.S. Constitution and its amendments.

COURT OF APPEALS. A court that reviews lower court decisions to insure that the law was correctly applied.

DEPOSITION. A written record of the testimony given by a witness who is questioned under oath outside the courtroom.

DETERRENT EFFECT. The belief that the threat of severe punishment will keep people from committing crimes.

EVIDENCE. Testimony, documents or objects introduced at a trial that prove or disprove a fact or facts.

EXECUTIVE BRANCH. The branch of government that enforces the law and administers its activities.

FELONY. A serious criminal act that can be punished by a prison sentence of more than one year, a fine, or both.

GRAND JURY. A jury that decides if a criminal case should go to trial after listening to the prosecution's evidence.

HUNG JURY. A trial jury that is unable to reach a unanimous verdict.

INDICTMENT. A written charge issued by a grand jury that orders the trial of a suspect for criminal conduct.

INJUNCTION. A court order that protects the rights of the plaintiff in a civil action by forbidding certain actions on the part of the defendant.

JUDICIAL ACTIVISM. The belief that the judiciary should take an active role in shaping the law to meet changing social needs.

JUDICIAL BRANCH. The branch of government that interprets the law.

JUDICIAL RESTRAINT. The belief that the judiciary should confine itself to a strict interpretation of the law.

JUDICIAL REVIEW. The power of the judicial branch to check the actions of the other two branches when they violate constitutional law.

JURISDICTION. The legal right of a court to hear a particular case.

LEGISLATIVE BRANCH. The branch of government that writes laws.

MISDEMEANOR. A minor crime, punishable by a fine, a prison sentence of one year or less, or both.

PAROLE. The early release of a criminal from prison.

PLAINTIFF. The party who sues for damages in a civil case.

PLEA BARGAIN. A deal in which the defendant in a criminal case agrees to plead guilty to a lesser charge in return for the dismissal of more serious charges.

PRELIMINARY HEARING. A court proceeding that determines whether there is enough evidence to hold a suspect for trial.

PROBATION. The early release of convicted criminals with the understanding that they can still be sent to prison if they violate the rules of their release.

REHABILITATION. The attempt to turn a criminal into a law-abiding citizen.

STATUTE LAW. Laws passed by the legislative branch of government.

SUBPOENA. A court order that requires a witness to appear in court to give testimony.

TORT. A wrongful act, injury or damage for which a civil action can be brought.

TRIAL JURY. The people selected at random from the community to decide criminal and civil cases after hearing the evidence.

VERDICT. The decision made by a jury after hearing the testimony in a court case.

Bibliography

Bernstein, Richard and Jerome Agel. *Into the Third Century: the Supreme Court.* Walker & Co., 1989

Carp, Robert and Ronald Stidham. *The Federal Courts.* Congressional Quarterly, Inc., 1985

Ernst, Morris L. *The Great Reversals*; *Tales of the Supreme Court.* Weybright & Talley, 1973

Goode, Stephen. *The Controversial Court: Supreme Court Influences American Life.* Julian Messner, 1982

Jackson, Donald Dale. *Judges: An Inside View of the Agonies and Excesses of an American Elite.* Atheneum, 1974

Koff, Gail J. *The Jacoby & Meyers Practical Guide to Everyday Law.* Simon & Schuster, 1985

Zerman, Melvyn Bernard. *Beyond a Reasonable Doubt; Inside the American Jury System.* Thomas Y. Crowell, 1981

Index

Picture Credits